Longing For
The Harmonies

poems by
Chuck Sullivan

Acknowledgments

Some of these poems have appeared in the
St. Andrews Review, The Greensboro Review,
Southern Poetry Review, Agora...

The cover is a painting by Emily T. Andress

Photo by Gene Houghey

ISBN: 0-93662-67-6

Printed by   Monument Printers & Lithographers, Inc.
                  Verplanck, New York
        for   St. Andrews Press
                  St. Andrews College
                  Laurinburg, North Carolina

Typesetting   Carol Tremblay Branner
& Design by   *Wordgraphics*
                  Wilmington, North Carolina

*For Pete and Aileen McGinty who gift me
with a room by the sea and the renewing grace of
The Laughing Place*

Contents

Longing For
The Harmonies

poems by

Chuck Sullivan

Longing for the Harmonies
—for Bob Kopf & Kevin Turner

This Fall not even one
shooting star soul is ghosting
off the pick and roll
nothing gives nothing goes
on the chipped coal asphalt
of McGuire's park
where time out of mind
we once courted Our Lady
of Rockaway Hoops
teeming with suitors
of three on three
in this salty cage by the sea

And alone I replay that day
a quarter century ago
when we three in low black "Cons"
found our mortal feet winged
as we rose in the blue leap
of air breezing above the sweep
of the roundball rookery flying
high with the half-court feather
touch of August excellence gliding
free of losses for three epic hours

Caught up in the tall dance of flesh
and shadows larger than life
our moves were the sweaty tunes
of our bodies keeping the once
in a lifetime time of the soaring
score of most arcing music
whose sphere would drop banked

lyric clean again and again to be
recalled through the past plunge
of a summer rim without a net
on a backboard with a deadspot
alive in the pressing sun's
most burning trophy won

By luck's all-stars shining
in the broad daylight skilled
in the hustling game of true fakes
a chance team of champions graced
with the free-lance fate
of friends becoming legends

In our own minds our hearts breaking
Time into song as we sang in our beers
like the sea in rim rounds
rounding the hoop of lost harmony

The Value of a Catholic Education

What it taught me a little was
to be
FBI is human to be
a priest just divine
to be a poet is to be
pitied unless grace saves you
from your dirty mind
but what I learned was Eternity

I learned it could be
dimly seen if you could imagine
one night when the moon cannot be stolen
every billion years or so a sparrow
brushing the tip of its infinite wing
on top of the Ark on Mt. Ararat
by the time the mountain was worn to a nub
Eternity would not have even begun

But then again forever could also be
I told myself when I was 16
the endless pause in the shudder between
confessing having beaten the Bishop
a finite number of times
and hearing the killing ice of my sins
melt into the living waters
of the Jordan cleansing me
in the forgiving fluency of a dead tongue

Out of the grace created in the seen
and unseen from the sun of God
I took to heart wisdom's shadow
from the Marists the Benedictines
the Sisters of St. Joseph and the Sacred
Heart itself something about the stone mind's
attachment to the dust we come from being

the dust we must return to which goodly
counselled by Our Lady led me to guess
that the sound of being One with the Father's
Hand clapping might just be the crucified
hush of the silent rain's secret reign
tapping the killing-met psalm
of the Buddha's tears
on my soul's windowed pain

Shantih, shantih, shantih, T.S. baby

And again and again a catholic Catholic
education from the root of Jesse *educare*
leads me to consider on the other hand
always open ever extended for us men
and for our salvation that the sound
of One Hand's Three Persons clapping
may really be what the Thunder of the grown
Child Jesus said with His hand whispering
to the dust whatever it was He wrote
just before He laid down

The New Law of sins and stones
putting first the bloodthirsty
in the last place of all of us
who in the end must wait equally
washed in the blood of the Lamb
at Heaven's Gateless Gate fooled
by the graceless wisdom of the serpent

Only to be saved by the elegant
foolishness of the Dove

As it was in the beginning
is now and ever shall be
world without end. Azen

Abbey Scholars: Spring River Singers

"Young men of fairest promise
who begin life upon our shores."
— Emerson, *The American Scholar*

When we were young men
boys of fairest promise
the funwheel spun
in the healing sun
of out classes

And college was cured
to a scholarly few Gypsy souls
Gitlow Redzo Butts Mr. George Doc
Dongus Tinkerbelle O'C The Whale
and The Hammer innocent of books
schooled in beer enrolled
on the other Abbey's pier

Drinking in the brightest
lager of the rare day's lesson
quaffing suds with Harp Rat Dirt Swan
Torso Beauty Superhead Whiskey Legs
Chairface Six O'Clock Pigeon Clapper
Hank Stank All American and God

Only knows who else was there
Southeast of Eden among the street-wise
and field-bright souls of Yankees
and Rebels steeped in the deep tight
blue and gray Spring brew
of the chaliced day

Congregating we were a host of Catholic
iconoclasts cast in the double spell
of the Big and small C
hoisting the communion of cool ones
we toasted within
our oddball legion of decency

Such a risky class act
of shirtless sun and river spirits
of the Mystical Body currently bent
on earning April's brief uncertain degree

Clearly conferred out of the fuzzy Blue
Ribbon dreams drafted in the good
wide open book of Who's Who
between the river and the sky

Where no one great or small
fails at all in speaking their heart
to sing the soul of an inland sea

The Pit of Sacred Heart

When April was the crudest month
breeding the oily slick
of love which would come
too soon to outline the world
I found myself an Abbey
boy trapped in the Passion
Pit of Sacred Heart
suffering the agony of soul

Kisses in the damp clutch of dry
loving the barely undone Spring
Queen in the Lenten vestibule
of the panting convent school

In her mouth irredeemably Catholic
I spoke in succoring tongues
of fallen angels filling my spirit
with the tinkling cymbals
of what my flesh was singing
in the swelling psalm of my blood's
firm bloom rising to the occasion
of sin still zipped
against the organdy wish
of the Queen's immaculate sundress
as I pressed the confession of my very
fabric's whisper to a spotted finish
in the Light-Bearer's race
against the black chaste click and clatter
of heels and beads climaxing the doom
of our curfew's little death

And verily the nun at the door
was the devil's Sister Incarnate
to the heavenly body of my earthly habit
to whom I bid godspeed
while she herded her sheep from the pit
past the Virgin and the crucifix
into the pink cloister of the Sacred Heart

From which I split into the outer darkness
my love's stain being mystery's map
of sin's just deserted island a mortal
atoll etched on the crease of my khakis
cleaving me to the early Easter edge
of Christ's first blood drawn
on the petal red ends
of the dogwoods lording over me
suffering their joy in the divine
wounds that sometimes always never heal

How We Spent Our Summer at
Governor's School East of Eden

We begin with God of course
taking a vacation
and under His Sunday wing
He leaves us to our own designs
to figure our grace in His
and so we live within the society
of dead poets who never die
indeed are Shelley's very
unacknowledged legislators
of the expanding universe

By St. Andrews grace daily
in deepest darkest Laurinburg
we seek crossing the First Causeway
the Prime Mover's Necessary Being
cast upon the lake of Carolina light
and on College Day you all dreamed
of being myths and legends
at Alma Maters that had not yet
borne you but for your dreams

And today in assembly the gifted
multitude waxed wise and poetic
on the potential and actual fate
of Nature's disposable images
the loss of a river here a river there
here a river there not a river
Heraclitus says you can't put your foot
in the same part of the river twice anyway
so what's the big deal Buddy just row
so what's the death of a couple of rain
forests among friends of the earth
no man is an island baby
but let's not get carried away
let's get *real* whatever that is

I mean what's with the Madonna
and Dick Tracy trying to solve the mystery
of why The Gods Must Be Crazy
in the face of the Fantasy Journey
within the Labyrinth of the most difficult
nuclear facility breeding simply the fallen
fruit of Adam's chain reaction that links
us here in the Gathering Place of the particular
general dance of form and matter
in love with wisdom's choreography of all souls
serenading their bodies to the strains
of Me and My Shadow trapped in joy's dance
reflecting duality mirrored on the walls
of Plato's Café where the real things served
got to be good looking 'cause they're so hard to see

And yet when the philosopher's cape
as white as the oxen Pythagoras offered
the Muses for his theorem unfurls
we spy Augustine's words stitched
in red upon its wings of how
"Love calls us to the things of this world."

Looking at Frost in a New Way

At the reading in the Gathering Place
the young girl about to read Frost
says she has brought nothing of her own
but will read three of his if she could

"Stopping By The Woods on a Snowy Evening"
"The Road Not Taken"
and "Design"

Slowly she caresses
the cover of the Collected Frost
Opens the book bends the page back
over the spine tilts her head to the right
and brings the poem as close to her face
as if she was about to tease it with a kiss
her eyes begin to finger the words
like braille's heartfelt sight
and the child speaks
and we read her silently

Good God how can she be so nearly blind
and make us see with such amazing grace
how well she held in the closest custody
of her eyes the woods the snow the road
the spider the moth and the heal-all
so close to her face and ran them over
her eyes for us to see in intimate scan
as she saw those words form into deeds

Giving us promises beyond sleep
with dreams to see before they keep
with dreams to see before they keep

Somewhere ages and reading hence
I will be telling of her sight with a sigh
two touching eyes made a vision of three poems
and let us see anew what we took for insight
and that is the grace of her difference

What but design of light when it falls
if light governs in a sight so small.

Climbing the Corporeal Ladder

In the grace of his company
we labor lost
in love's work ethic
more skilled than we could imagine
He toils beside us like one of our own
the most complete union man
finishing what would have alone killed
any of us working stiffs

Of course He is about the business
of His Father who owns the whole
big shebang lock stock and Spirit
and still the babe started out
at the bottom
of the corporeal ladder
and rose to the top
from within working like hell
in failing He succeeded
and giving the devil his due
He climbed even higher
and won the final rung
a job well done for all of us
even though He didn't owe us
a god damned thing
and had absolutely nothing to prove

For all us workers in the vineyard
the Ascension was the end
and the beginning of a good career move
with the Son finding Himself
right back where theology started
at the right hand of the Father

Who said nice guys finish last
when the last shall be first
and the first shall be last

The Steamy Release of Easter

It's hot as hell
across the border in the heat
of the Juarez morning growing
no joy on us stuck between Good
Friday and Easter Sunday
looking to score a little
something to ease the Holy

Saturday pain of Jesus Descending
into Hell we find ourselves paying
customers in the inner sanctum
of the barrio where only the best
houses are adorned
with fly-latched blankets for doors

And there knock was open wide
to the emptiness inside
the tomb where Coronado the cabby
our guide had sent us to get high
and so stoned we rolled away
martyrs of escape having copped
for a song some of the White
Lady's heady lines whose up
pulled us down to the gravity
of the grace in the apparition
way at the end of the truth
in the dust of the street

An old lady all black widowed-out
and sonless growing in her mourning
like dark light straight from the trunk
of Death's tree bent limb from limb to life

And behind her I see squatting
one of the neighbors we must love
as ourselves relieving himself of us
and left there at great price
in the Holy Saturday sun human waste
shines beyond belief waiting
for the steamy release of Easter

The Weather Above the law

"For what man knows the will of God
or who can conceive what the Lord intends?"
—*Wisdom 9:13*

Could the Kingdom of God
be likened unto the bootlegger
within who when faced with being
low on the regular stuff
divined to deliver a special sop
and brewed his truth up
out of anti-freeze
and whatever else was lying about
his hidden still

And then as if told
he ran his white lightning
out on Thunder Road hauling
its crackling spirits down
from the mountain just spoiling
to haunt souls
like the weather above The Law

And when he arrived
straightway it was night
and what he did he did quickly
and his buyers having not
read the face of the sky
thought he was wise
in overlooking everything
save being true

To supplying his faithful
each soul appointed to hold
a thirst ready for surprise
and for this cause
they came unto that hour

Where in the substance
of the kick hoped for
each believer knocked back
the evidence of things not seen
and so verily the with Bands
and Beauty on their tongues
some were blessed with blindness
and others only died
some for the dead to bury them
and others merely to be born again

Later at home above
the still his heart being
where his treasure is the bootlegger sage
having heard the Word
of the bad news
was simply moved to play
Iscariots's old saw
about how they pay you
your wages you take
your chances with Death

You sin I sin we sin they sin
all I can say is it's a livin'

You drink what you drink
It makes the Son of man think

Fixing the Dark

In the street-wise chapel
of my child's behold
mystery darted in guardian
sparks from the arc
welder's hand and danced
in swarms of random thrones
and powers about the floor
like light from light begotten
not made of one being chanced

Within the shop of Principalities
next door to nanny's and poppy's
where looking in the window
I could not see what I knew
was being fused to fix the dark
with the fireflies of surprise

And later that very day
when my East Side sun
was growing old and scraping
the sky beyond the empire
state of my building and beyond
the Hudson too upon whose
tides the Half-Moon once sailed
there was no place to go then

But up to the roof and catch
the rise of it all going down
as I hid near where the pigeons
like Seraphim and Cherubim were
cooped save when grace blessed
them loose from the hands
of the ancient of day's end
the hood of whose windbreaker
cowled the full face
I would never see as my eyes rose

To entertain these pigeon-winged
strangers into being a flock
of Angels and Archangels
committed lover by lover
in the covenant of their shadows
to not being above the Virtues
of staking claims on the fire-escaped
windows as they counted the uncommitted
sins of all souls embodied
in the common mystic precincts
of St. Stephen's parish
and then making light of
the flashing witness in their
wings I saw them write the one
wordless name's streak of all
the neighborhood's unsung saints
in the Manhattan hymnal
of my heart's fallen dark
choiring it there like an open secret
solved upon the star-riddled air

Something New Under the Sun

"I believe because it is absurd."
                                    Tertullian

The morning-fresh tabernacle
always at home in missionary territory
holy rolls its way past the cornerstone
of the Faith on Trade and Tryon
and stacked in it loaves of Sunbeam
bread wait to be transformed
into the Word made Flesh
and deep in his cups of the blood

Of the new and everlasting covenant
the old whiskey priest forever
according to the Order of Melchisidech
and "The Power and the Glory"
blesses what crosses his path
and mumbles as the van rumbles by
Hoc est corpus meum...
just like in the old days
before they turned
the victim and celebrant around
and graced in that moment
we are all contemporaries
of the quick Christ gathered
on a consecrated corner in Charlotte, North Carolina

And so with all children of light
suddenly delivered by the substance
and accidents the Sunbeam driver
feels beyond belief
that he is indeed powered by what is
rising within the beginningless
something new under the sun

the daily bread we live by alone
baked while we sleep
and given in the Body and Blood
to be eaten in the wilderness
speeding heaven-bent toward all
the Sacrament's stories that have not
sold out the Lord
outside the Gates of Eden

The Roundtripping Charm of Distance

"Fides ex audita."
—*St. Paul*

Around the warm-up of our Zenith's glow
Poppy and I would pepper with clubhouse
Talk as we caught the Rockaway fireflies
broadcasting to our porch the scoring
torches of their report each flicker
flashing the tiny night game's needlepoint
of our Giant stars shining on the distant
diamond of their radio do or die road game

Play by playing their August hearts
out to us from the tower across the river
and not from St. Louis
the tickings of their innings coming in
sight unseen pictured in the perfect
voice of Les Keiter pitching us
the re-created game's lies that became
the runs hits and errors of the truth
sparkling in off the wire

Calling them like he saw them
at the ballpark inside his head
we too heard and saw what he said
the sizzler up the middle
splitting the keystone sack
the line drive to dead center
the Baltimore chop to the hot corner
the Texas Leaguer and the long fly
back back back back boom off the wall
the blast into the stands
and the quick glove everywhere stranding
in its lyric web a treasure

of pocketed hits copped in the killing
of a rally each play taken on the blind
faith of re-creation proclaimed in one
great grandstanding play after another
whose most effecting sound was braille
dial-lit on the radio's air
that kept us in touch with the game
lived to be reckoned in the records
of my boy soul's universal pastime

Played that night inside the Zenith
light of the crucial bungalow dark
when the full count of the world's
porch hung on the yet to be thrown
fate of Time's Cardinal curve
already served to Say Hey Willie Mays
and lifted of a past sudden out
of the present heart of the order
and shot into the seventh heaven's
close final score of the stars
like the moon's roundtripping
charm of distance

Little Boy Blue

> "...for dust thou art
> and unto dust thou shalt return."
> —*Genesis 3:19*

The little toy lamb is red with rust
But sturdy and staunch he stands
And the little toy shepherd is mantled in dust
And the child's flock molds in his hands

In the fulness of time the shepherd was new
And the lamb was Passover fare
And that was the time Judas kissed Little Boy Blue
Because Scripture had scripted them there

"Now don't you go 'til I come back," He said,
"And make you a joyful noise!"
So trundling off to His dogwood bed
He dreamt of the dead burying the dead
And all of His pretty toys

And as we were dreaming an angel song
Awakened our Little Boy Blue
And from His Easter and Ascension
The Years are many the years are long
Yet the real toys are souls staying true

And they wonder waiting the long years through
In the dust love makes of fear
What has become of our Little Boy Blue
Since He kissed us and put us here?

Yet faithful to Little Boy Blue we stand
Each alive in the same old place
Secrets changed to mysteries awaiting
The touch of The Child's nailed hand
The smile of His crucified face

The Bones of the Dead Child

There is dust on top of the world
I am up against today
the elementary globe of Riley School
which I spin Imagination's
unschooled spy that I am

Across the room Daniel Boone
is showing some pioneers around
a torn frontier on the peeling wall
and here in the 5th grade
I am a man on the frontier too

Having stolen a page from Arp
and wishing the children to eat it
I tempt them to tell themselves
exactly what does the dream of Eggs
as Big as Houses Dancing taste like

Then next we will create ten things
that could never happen like a piano
holding the keys to the Kingdom
touching on the open
secret of the poem's lie
that tells the truth leading us
on to the image in a class by itself

That pictures what the ungraded
heart of Truth and Beauty is really
like until its loveliness almost
fades into a recess

Bell tolling just loudly enough
to rattle awake
the bones of the dead

Child alive in a well inside me

The Clown and the Crow Run Away
From the Circus

Once upon a time between
being under the heels of stepfathers
dreaming of being a clown
the young son sat on the sagging porch
his features bleached in the natural
white-face of a child's grief grinning
to set the world afire
with the cry of laugh's desire
waiting for his Mom to be rolled home
from the Unicorn Café
where her friend Sir Tom tends only bar

Still waiting still waiting
he saw himself in slow motion cutting
fool through three shows as the star child
clown of The Greatest Show On Earth
all the little children absolutely cracked-up
when he unpacked his heart
from the tiny jammed car all clowns must break
out of alive and it just killed the people
when he threw a bucket of paper water
all over them after having fled the burning
house in the dark that fell at the last show's end
when across the street the Mobil horse
in flight flashed its red neon wings
and the Arrow cab struck home

It was then his startled heart heard
his mother's quivering curbside show
her voice crackling once more the ringmistress
static of her bring 'em back alive attraction
and in a shot the child clown hooked his eyes
with the clarity of a crow's stare

on the beastly shape that leapt to hold her
until he saw the lost and found beauty
of his own flesh and blood slip
from her keeper's grip and stumble toward him
and almost reaching him fumble and drop
in a Mom pratfall her purse spilling the loose
presents of small change at his feet

And so suddenly paid the clown's crow-shadow
took pain's mime of wings
and fled in dark flutter
around the back of the broken Big Top
dovetailing into the hanged angels
of laundry splitting their sides
on his mother's untended line

The Child Who Begs to Differ

Brothers and Sisters nothing is
impossible with God
so come let us imagine
the child all dolled up
in the fulness of time
at the foot of the tree
the swaddled babe who beggared
in prophecy begs to differ with death

O' come let us imagine for real
Mary and Joseph the shepherds
the wise men the angels
the little drummer boy
even the ox and ass
keeping time in the stable
beneath the Redeemer's elegant star
all making hay while The Son
of Man shines in the manger

O' come let us imagine for keeps
the Prince of Peace the First Cause free
of all sins' effects too good to be true
ever being never not being if He wasn't
truly God moved in His prime by the will
of freest design to be grown up on

The Christmas Tree
found bare in Spring
of all lights save
The Light of the World
the essential ornament
of His Mystical Body
hung with the merciful care
of His own Divine Hand

By which we too overshadowed
by the power of the Most High
must have all our hearts' labors
give birth to the crowning absurdity
and be ready to nurse in our souls
the faith-filled surprise of the Christ

The Child who will lead us
into the infinite Easter
of the long promised land
where we know all will be
calm all will be bright
on that day of the Lord
            Alleluia!
that is coming
like a thief in the night

Once Upon a Time Happily Ever After

Once upon a time

In the fulness of time
in the Kingdom come beyond
the magic of the cartoon
empire of the creator
of Snow White and Sleeping Beauty

>   Day breaks
>   Night falls
>   Time flies
>   The Star shines
>   The Child is born
>   The angels sing
>   Truth is Beauty
>   Beauty is Truth
>   Sin begins
>
>   To end in truth is
>   Consequences that lie
>   In the manger
>   On the Main Street
>   Of Creation

Where we and Magi find
the swaddled coin of the soul's realm
in the new born currency of the ransomed
ransoming Babe the price of whose life
is not weighed in the balance
of the silver nor counted in the gold
of the Child we all must grow up to be
who does not live and die and rise
by bread alone but

Happily ever after

The Key to Geometry

In the Kingdom
of the circle
of our infinite friend

Where the circumference
is nowhere
and the center everywhere

If we pay attention
a hidden radius may be ours

A radiant tightrope
we may dance upon

While the angel rounds
of the line
curved about us sing

Berries on Bloomsday: For Linda

All the while
the mystery of it all
is being solved within
our white mischief's
arresting dark in which
sparks fly in the stolen
tick and hidden tock
of kiss and touch killing
matinee time with innocent
crimes of fled scenes
and juicy finales

And escaping we make it
home clean to quaff suds
pick ribs make a sweet mess
soak up Ulysses Hamlet & Dedalus
all of whom from one book
make we two blush
like berries on Bloomsday
hanging above Molly's bed
as we fall to the swell blazes
boiling our souls' body heat

Where in the church
of our hearts
the choir is on fire
singing the feast
of our consuming heat
hymning ashes to ashes
and dust to dust
from lust we come
and to love we must return

Praising a universe of yes yes yes
as if we had no no no other Joyce

One of Many Heart Tricks

Tristans what you need is
a slippery pearl of great price
and a beaker of acid
but
a sugar cube
and a glass of water
will do for some

Then beckon a beautiful creature
and hand that Isolde her cube
then in the flirt
of your tricky heat
ask her to draw
a simple design
perhaps of precise need
a heart with your initials on it

Flash a smile and take the cube
flourish it then drop it
in the glass of water
invite the lovely thing
to concentrate on her palms
then with the greatest care
take her hands and holding them
over the troubled water
blow upon them
like the wind over
"Oed' und leer das Meer"

And then for the grand finale
let her hands go
and there appearing on her palm
is the sign of your initialed heart
seemingly
drawn to her from the vanished cube

And in that sugared moment
without a doubt
she is yours for life
and maybe forever
if
indeed your sleight-of-hand
has pulled the trick off right

Pan Meets the Paraclete

Wherever two or three
are gathered alone
in the name of small change
all that cometh is vanity
in the booth of the Joy

Adult bookstore dark
where I feel not
my soul's song of songs
but the hot eye
of that dirty old man

Pan keeping sweaty watch
upon some fleshy green
where a tattooed son
of the peeping god
pants unsure

As any doubting tomcat
his fluted member cuddly
and thick as a baby's
arm being borne
by one nymph's less
than mothering hand

In & out
of the succoring red
mouth of the Mystical

body of the totally
Other dark-
rooted blonde Temple
of the Holy

Ghost with pimples
on her ass

Last First Love

Out of the wing-folded
readiness for surprise
the cell opens

Like a swan accepting
a vow to couple
its heart with one mate

Forever
that is the beginning
of life conceived

In the divine act
of Love's last first love
chastely souled in the kiss

Of the free willing flesh
of the freshly ravished monk

The Wheel of Fortune Changes
Channel & Time
—August 6, 1990

Out of the inscrutable blue
dropped on the paid-for air
of an August pacific nowhere

Flashes on us the sharp resolution
of Toshiba's Blackstripe tube
into which without thinking we fall

Back into our living rooms and find
a rip-off of The Grateful Dead
leading us on to believe
that they like Reagan are moonlighting
now for the Empire of the Sun

Their mission to Keep On Truckin'
the karmic props
of The Wheel of fortune
across channels and Time

Driving home the commerce of change
chanced on History's game show

The Last Wild Once and Future Irish Rose
—For Mary Doherty

Now no Mick bars roar
and no terrible beauty is born
on every changed street
in the wintered heart
of Rockaway's summer city
and even the once bungalowed beach
has sunk to a sky-scraped seashore

By the Belle harbor window
of my mother's blessed in green room
between the ocean and the bay
I take you in seeming alone to be
the same ancient songbird Queen

Who still rules if light lies
and make-up tells the truth
Herself royal and unaltered
in the era of airs before
Rock 'n Roll was king
the reigning nightingale
serenading in an exiled land
castled in a gin mill
christened "The Cave"

And though in truth its graffiti
ruins lie now waiting to be
or not to be developed
across from the dying amusement
park which the children must
enter through the clown's mouth
you picture "The Cave" as it was
and say you say still grows there
older but unfading the last wild
once and future Irish Rose blooming

in that little bit of heaven that fell
from out the sky one day this side
of the ocean where always
the wee folk keep at play

In your voice and the power
of your touch to trace the charm
of remembrance in the finger dance
upon the Baby Grand's brogued keys
a lilting pure and tinkling tune
as if the emerald murmurs
of the elves themselves were enchanting
with a haloed spell the bar's pale
spotlight around you into being
the moon's Irish Duet of body and soul

Lost in found song
as fair as The Rose of Tralee
as haunting as Molly Malone

Radio Hanoi is Still Playing Our Song

When I need you in my arms
When I want you
And all your charms
Whenever I want you
All I have to do is dream
of you deep in the search

And destroy peace
of your toss and turn suburban night
my lost flight found flying apart again
my nuclear family exploding once more
in the forgetful skies
of your starless wifely sleep

And a prisoner of my dream's war
I storm yours a rank and numbered
spirit on broken wings appearing
in the taunting float of my chained
fall to drop untouched through the flak
of the black widow sky you have webbed
about the unfaithful hunch
of your own grave needs

In which I lie buried less
than an angel only a flyer grounded
in the strands of a limbo menace
my absent presence beaten to a dread
hero's ghost of a chance prayed for
and against only to be waked
in a living hell of the maybe dead
of fates left up in the battle's air
a soul without benefit of a body bag

Do I dare think my love
that your occupied heart is
like some dink village
I must destroy in order to save
my memory from being laid
to husbanding rest in the piece
missing in the action
you get from the new peacekeeper
whose heat-seeking entreaties
you now harbor in that tropic hazard
where once you tucked me in

And though you may want me only dead
or alive with some slope concubine
I will live at least forever

Alone in the sleep shallow air
of your fallen evening
the shot-down pilot
the aced-out hawk
with no choice but to fly nightmare
strikes through the turncoat skies
of your heart's brainwashed dreams

Bye Bye now my love long overdue
we are all vaguely accounted for
just listen my dove
Radio Hanoi is still playing our song

Evacuating the Island

When they killed the power
even the diehards fled Hilton Head
in a head-lit cortege
of Beamers and Jags jockeying
for position on the straight and narrow
of the only road leading off the island

In the driving rain of the bumper
to bumper calm before the storm
of the killer hurricane Hugo
driven horns raged at each shudder
in the herding pulse of the pilgrim
shuffle toward higher ground

And when dead in their tracks
my rusting wheels died
the best Samaritan in the Benz
behind me shunted my old Malibu
off on the median
and in that downpour I was no man

To be stopped for on the dwindling
island's side of the road humming
the Cascades' "Rhythm of the Rain"
reading Kerouac and telling my green
bone Irish beads like any stranded
child of Mary in a pinch would pray

A good three hours later
with all the island gone
I helped a trooper hook his cables
so he could cook me
with the kindness of some state juice

At first the gift failed to catch
Faith's reflex in stalled things
but then old Jude on the dash
may have mercied a spark or two
when I turned the key felt night
fall and the hopeless case
of an engine roar powering me to thank
the trooper and take small pride
in prizing I was the last one leaving

Until suddening right through me
shining toward the shelter of the storm
I spied the bright lights of the Reaper's
limo-sleek pick-up slipping its grave
way past me into my mirror winding down
the straight and narrow of the Kingdom
already come but not yet here in which
all objects may be closer than they appear

Putting on the Gulag

Ike was on the greens
at Burning Tree
and Stalin was putting
on the Gulag
purging all his birdies
with the dead-eye skill
of The Hammer & Sickle

When the Pro made a club
of his country and smiled
at friend and foe not a soul
escaped his love of the game
and at his mercy in the clutch
the Chilling Hacker ice water
in his veins carded them nameless
beat them like a drum
and drove them into the cold
blood's ground for the glory
and the kingdom of his name

Nyet's sudden death was yes
to Big Brother's play-off power
and while he played through
every unplayable lie he could
find Mother Russia's greens
ran Red on the Siberian links
of her brainwashed minds

This comrade took the grave fairways
of his own design to heart
and in the course
of history's dear life
became the czar of tee & slice

At the shank of his will
heads rolled to the non-person
holes like dented balls
pitted with eyes
and like any shady duffer
in hell he would fudge a few

Million strokes and club
his cult across the leader board
while out of the 19th hole
The Voice of America played
"Shake, Rattle and Roll"

Conjugating the Verb To Be Or Not To Be
With Much Ado About Nothing

To be or not to be

The whether 'tis nobler or not verb
with much ado about nothing
save everything conjugated infinitely says

Before Abraham was

I am	who am a mystery	Am I not?
You are	What is a secret	Adon't you know?
he is	she be love's verb trip	Adon't they do it, though?

We are	us who be a miracle	Adon't you dig it?
You are	we what be a trick	Adon't you get it?
They are	them who don't know shit	Ain't they dead as we be quick?

I guess so sweet Prince if only
you we and all the angels
singing you to sleep be or not be
putting it in the waking form
of an answer that goes not
a little something like this

What it is   What it is   or whatever

What it is   What it is   or whatever   That is

That is the question
                mark for and against us
                                        even in silence
As we speak
                the sound and the fury
                                signifying nothing new
Save the zero in the number one
                        Grace of what be the happy fault
Of sin's Originality

A Bowler Perhaps:
—for Samuel Beckett

Long brevity the soul
of Death to the doubting
Thomas a Beckett briefly
says no less is more while
Time is out of order
in attendant Godot
where waiting bones echo
Tertullian Woody Allen
and The Flying Wallendas
cheeping cheek to cheek
i believe because it is
absurd that 90% of Death
is just showing up
or is it the other way
around in any circus case
keep in mind too
that for the body
Death is on the wire
all else is waiting
for...well...you know
nothing really I guess
except what I am absolutely
relatively sure of
which is that God definitely
in all probability
maybe if She shows up
wears without a doubt
the shadow hat of
a bowler perhaps

So be ye on the lookout

A Decent Hour
—for Saint Jack

In the beginning
toward the very end of it all
in the middle of the dead of night
approaching the plank where all the angels
dove off into the holy void
you find out Kerouac in Time

That not even an old friend
and lover not even oddly enough
The Holy Goof's old squeeze Carolyn
cares to pull up a cross-country chair

And pour a long distance glass
of wine and just listen one more time
to your soul beat its way as you say

Your sing improvising
the bop eschaton shadow
of last things hitching
its quest across the coast
to coast wires that connect nothing
Into something where loss will be lost
but all she can do is pretend
that it's the connection and not
the friend that's gone ghostly

And then she shrouds some sad
transparency on you like, "Jesus, man,
it sounds like you're in Siberia!

Look, Jack, this is just impossible!
Why don't you hang up and call back

At a decent hour."

Strangers and Angels: A Novena
—for Diane Arbus

"Be not forgetful to entertain strangers:
for thereby some have entertained angels unawares."
—*Hebrews 13:2*

"Be not forgetful to entertain
strangers..." in the thorny bed
of roses we make and must lie in
where there are no pillows
to cushion disaster and where once
in the middle of making love
at that snapping moment of giving
and taking when everything falls
into place you pictured yourself
forgiving your parents for having
conceived you and like any innocent
all your life experienced in returning
to the scene of the crime guilty of a secret
about a secret focused in the art of the split
second in which you found your conscience
to be the shuttered apology machine
for your soul to make amends within
the cock-eyed truth of your trembling lens

II

All tied up in the freedom of the unthinkable
you were as free as any saint like Teresa
by Bernini who carved the ecstasy of her flesh
in infinitely spirited stone your heart too
was all enbarbed with love that let you eye
the peculiar grace of sinners through
a seized stained glass asking
in your awed field of depth
Who can I go home with?
Who is it that can tell me who I am
in the glossy cauldron of black and white
where my shy charms meant no harm
passion could not be charged with?

III

Once I dreamt in the red whispers
of darkroom advice
for you to shoot me silver me print me
with your light and stain me brightly
in the lightning strike
of your jagged sights wedding me
to the cutting edge of the lively
private property of every face
correctly seen as being the beautiful bloom
of beauty and beast not conformed to this world
but transformed by the renewing
of things honest in the sight
of never taking a body for a soul

IV

In its exposing shudder
your eye was tattooed with the view
that the center of the razor
is scarred at the blade's edge
of your cropped blood's
cuts in search of the certain slice
of feeling that fails the faith
in believing that giving someone
else your soul really does have
its benefits though as each close-up
shows even lovers cannot put on
each other's skins and that no matter
how hot or cold you may moan
no one else's joy or pain is made
to be a copy of your own

V

Caught in the act
of bringing to light the hidden
not the evil but the forbidden
mystery of the clear facts you lived
revealed in the shots of rare faces
grained with wild counsel
from which there was no turning
back or away you would be reborn
and you would die again and again
in love with the camera whose passion
was to appear it never lied
in capturing freely how freaks
are the perfect looney mirror
a crazy brittle glass
of the soul's aristocracy
in which there is succor
born every minute as Our Lady
of the Sideshow prays us to say

VI

In the harboring of your gaze
you sought to frame how everyone suffers
the singular burden of being nothing
if the film of all your secrets is exposed
secrets like your window undressing worship
in which you would caress and love yourself
in front of God and those neighbors
who watched your moving solo tableau
and would have loved to have loved you
to death as you loved yourself
closing your eyes to conjure the rock 'n squeal
shadow of the subway flasher as he took
your picture with his hand-held gadget and fled
what could you feel touching your camera obscura
your fingers flying like you were clicking
off shot after shot in the quick of time exposed
were you a night owl shaking as you came
with one hand perched on the dreamy sill
what could you feel what could you feel
but the juice of the wound that never heals

VII

In a lifetime of cleansing
the high windows of the soul
when you were brought to earth
are your pictures all that's left
for us to tell if you were a jumper
or just a window washer who fell
protected and privileged
into the welcoming net of arms
linking you with bag ladies
the little people the headless man
the Jewish Giant Congo the Jungle Creep
the boy with the toy grenade
the half-man half-woman Moondog
the Mystic Barber and Presto the Fire Eater

VIII

I wonder Diane in the night of the flesh
with no light for any snapshot souvenir
when you like so many of us now and again
mistook a stone for a heart
a body for a soul
did your pin of wings
bless you with flight's amulet
over the little death
of sex granting your body
an out of soul experience
that lets you feel the hard core
of someone else's little death
being an easy way out of your own life

IX

On the roll's last shadow-proof
you kept your word
and slipped a print
of Kandinsky's death mask
under the door of a neighbor
you had promised it to and then
you went back to your apartment
locked the door and sat
for your self-portrait hooked
on the leering eye of Death himself
who like any porn king
fat with pinky rings
loves to make his living by treating
us to pose as things
and make rot of our ecstasy

Anyway Diane all along even in the end
life was the secret you were dying to do
like when your friend came each month
in a rush of blood
and you glorified in its flow
so on the last day true to form
and most dramatic composition
you let hurry from your slit

Wrists the final period's rotogravure
of death and life where all pictures
are pictures of light in the fix
of whose even darkest chamber
"... some have entertained angels unawares."

Why the Scarecrow Lost His Girlfriend

Having lost his girlfriend Regina
in the random

Universe where God does not play
dice the lover chanced
by choice to marry himself
off to the Lord of the Dance

Whose eerie choreography
led him to be
the hunchback standing tall
in rags of awe and flesh and bone
among the workers in the vinyard

Soren the scarecrow on fire
with fine eyes like diamonds
set to cut the looking glass
of the soul wise
as a serpent innocent
as a dove crying over and over
Either/Or Either/Or

At the Zen black and white birds
of Heaven's pecking appetite
as they rose and dove
in fear of love's airy dialectic
of lyric wings circling above the trembling

Field of the good and bad seed
fallen on the either
fertile or fallow ground
of our Being
harvested or not from within

The sky's dark quick
when either the storm comes up
or not like the scorn
of Swift for abstract minds

And finds Soren standing there
the fool on the hill of skulls exactly
still begging for lightning
humbled by the rain
who stuck in his Faith leaps
to grow into the warning
vigil of his roots

The Ascent of Man

With the mascots running amok
at the sold-out Coliseum
in the Queen City of N.C.
at a time out of joint
at the NBA All-Star Game
we strike up the music
counting their dead to beat our band

And while oh by gosh by jingo
the All-Star strategy is plotted
to the strains of Lee Greewood's
Proud To Be An American
we see on The Big Picture above us
the instant replay of Desert Storm's
bombing of Baghdad lit up
like a Christmas Tree
just like they said on TV
ten days after the Epiphany

And so we pledged our allegiance
to the flag
of the United States of America
and to the Republic
for which it stands
one nation under God
with liberty and justice for all

Being dragged on a long pole
round and round the Coliseum floor
by Hugo the Hornet working the crowd
up to a fever buzz of making
the world safe for monarchy
while the Phoenix Suns' Gorilla slam
dunks off a tiny trampoline

and grabbing hold of his goal
pulls himself up by natural selection
to stand beating his chest proud
to be an American
mascot on the back of the rim
of Pandemonium reigning supreme

With the Hornet as he hands Old Glory
up to the Gorilla on the rim
who wraps himself in the flag
of Everyman ascended there

Meanwhile at home
armed with the smart bombs
of the Rising Sun's TVs
patriots in La-Z Boys
zap the doors of missile plants
and the schools of infidels
all hell breaking loose by remote control

on the ruins of the Garden of Eden

Early Spring on Sullivan's Island

Above the lamb whitecaps of March first
that break and lie down with the lion
of the sun in the peaceable
kingdom of Sullivan's Island

The wanton rainbow kites dart
and dip the spectrum swirl
of their tails flirting with the broad
daylight wink of the black
and white lighthouse trailing
their colors like the ghost guessed will
of God Noah knew by heart

And out of that House of Light
in the flash of its beehive spent
in knowing the world
in the Biblical sense Spring falls
early breaking us
on through to the other side

Of the darkly refined sky
of the cease fire above the rubble
of the Garden where the serpent
has his field day and where now
diplomats are hawking doves

And there we find in the cornered
curved and spinning temple of the new world
order fresh as Spring early fallen
from grace for the victors
and Muslims for better or worse
that in all war's pieces
of lions and lambs
the dead always
come home first and last

Walking on Water: In Memory of My Mother

"Walking on water wasn't done in a day."
—Jack Kerouac

Cater-cornered to the crack
house in the hospital that lies
tucked in the ruins of Rockaway
lifeless now as lifetimes of summer
suckingly ebbed and gone to seed
you were healed
and died leaving alive
the doctors mystified
who not having known Mom
how well you sung the old songs
could not for the life of them
find the fine unseeable swan
you had sewn in your heart

My sister your daughter Mary Ann
kept her grown-up little girl's vigil
in Intensive Care and in your spasms
she held your legs and carressed
their shakes with a mothering stillness
and when your parched need baffled speech
she graced you to write the word WATER
on a slate the first word Helen Keller
touched to her Ann Sullivan our Ann Sullivan
scratched to her daughter and she like a cooling
wing angeled a wet cloth to bless your lips
with a taste of the slaking to come

I too watched the night in ICU
and left on the table beside the bed
your keys of the Kingdom
found on the face
of "The Clowns of God"

the God into whose final arms
you flew fully knowing the rush
of the truth in the beauty of how
He is nobody's clown
and everybody's perfect fool

II

Dying for a drink
with our Belle Harbor hearts beached
Mary Ann cousin Mike and I
like children of all ages
sifting through the deadweight
of sundown sand find ourselves
in your room neat as a pin
cramped as a confessional
sorting through what's left
of your twilight's last effects

The very clothes off your back
the winter things the summer items
that gray blazer I last saw you off in
and last of all Death's unmentionables
each sheer thing flawlessly folded
we donated it all to St. Francis
who once in life Mom was
as naked as you are now Mom
when you see him just ask him

And your table bed and clock
like the bell book and candle
of good magic we will to some unknown one
some young lady the Super tells us
will be moving in tomorrow Mom
on whose head dances the countless
choirs of angels moving tomorrow into
your room Mom as empty as the Easter tomb

Mary Ann steadied by Michael's hand
packed your pictures of us framed
like black and white saints
altared in mock stained-glass
like the flawed icons we are
of experienced children most innocently
loved with great Faith beyond belief

Of the books I sent you I leave
"Final Payments" for the next tenant
that some unknown one young lady
and take to heart with me "The Wheat
That Springeth Green" I carry away too
the books of my poems and find in my
catechism of hearts that no matter what
the lions dream of vanishing species Mom
you are at last the mother who is
the child at rest who makes belief
real in the juggler on the radio

And then all three of us sweating
and struggling for air fled
with our living treasures crossing
ourselves to arrive at the bar
and toast you with Harps
inside the Irish Circle
of your makeshift wake tickling
our grieing fancies with the sad
blarney of your death
that was no death at all
only like a disappearance
into a starry tavern
where you are in fine shape
and never need struggle to sing
with an empty glass again
because you love God
and have a trick in you

III

Lifeguards on the Death Watch
having laddered to the throne
of the deserted chair looking out
over the dead of night's grave sea
from which all life rose
Mary Ann and I Mom hold on
each of us the other shivering
ourselves back to the young sun
of the old beach we once ruled
as your children
in the burn of Rockaway light

And from our perch we see now wave
upon wave speaking to us like the tide
turning lyrics of the Lord choiring
they hymn that sings your phanthom
headstone Mom to be the seaward
charm of a fathomless psalm

And out of the sea's deep congregation Mom
come forth murmurs and rumors of murmurs
of your soul's fragile unbreakable flow
rolling in endlessly endless indivisible
waves whose muffled rumble runs
the final night's cursive coast
with the wide white-capped heartbeat
of your name changing under cover
of darkness in which the presence
of your absence grows round us
like the moon's pale majesty
of the Spirit's Law that lets you slip
from here to there and everywhere found
nowhere save in moving

Away across the holy sea
which we too must go to reach
the razored end of grief's horizon
where just like Bing sings Mom
the blue of the night
meets the gold of the day
where you will be that someone
there waiting for my sister and me

And so still keeping watch Mom
Mary Ann and I are your stranded
angels who in grace stray wise
with the pain of knowing
walking on water isn't done in a day

CHUCK SULLIVAN was born and raised in New York City. He attended Belmont Abbey College on a basketball scholarship playing for Al McGuire.

After college Chuck spent a year as a VISTA volunteer, working with migrant laborers in Florida and West Virginia. From 1967-76, Chuck served as Varsity Basketball Coach/Athletic Director and Chairman of Humanities at Bishop McGuinness High School in Winston-Salem, North Carolina.

Since 1976, he has been a poet-in-the-schools for the South Carolina Arts Commission, Cabarrus County and the Charlotte-Mecklenburg Schools. He has also been the NEA Poet-in-Residence at Butler University in Indiana.

Every summer since 1979, Chuck has taught poetry and philosophy at North Carolina Governor's School East.

Longing For The Harmonies is also the title of a documentary about Chuck that aired on PBS in 1989.

34
CH